Original title:
Stitched in Sunlight

Copyright © 2024 Creative Arts Management OÜ
All rights reserved.

Author: Vivienne Beaumont
ISBN HARDBACK: 978-9916-90-742-9
ISBN PAPERBACK: 978-9916-90-743-6

The Colors of Serenity

In shades of blue, the sky so vast,
Whispers of peace, the moments pass.
Gentle breezes through the trees,
A tranquil heart, a calm that frees.

Golden sun on fields of green,
Nature's canvas, pure and serene.
Petals dance in fragrant air,
Each hue a memory, sweet and rare.

Soft lavender at twilight's glow,
A symphony of colors slow.
In silence, colors weave their rhyme,
A timeless beauty, pure, sublime.

Embrace the hues, let worries fade,
In serene shades, a life well made.
Together we find, in every glance,
The colors of gentle, peaceful dance.

Nature's Radiance

Amidst the trees, the sunlight streams,
A haven filled with joyful dreams.
Whispers of wildlife, soft and clear,
Nature's song, a melody dear.

Mountains rise in regal stance,
Inviting hearts to take a chance.
Rivers flow with timeless grace,
Each ripple tells of sacred space.

Blossoms bloom in vibrant light,
Painting the world with pure delight.
Every petal a story told,
Of seasons changing, young and old.

In nature's arms, we find our way,
A radiant peace in every day.
Together we stand, hand in hand,
In harmony, on this blessed land.

Strokes of Dawn

A blush of pink on silent sky,
Whispers of light as stars slip by.
Awakening earth in gentle hues,
Nature's canvas, fresh morning views.

Birds take flight with morning's grace,
Chasing shadows in the vast space.
Each ray a promise, a day reborn,
Painting soft paths where dreams are worn.

Warmth Beneath the Clouds

In the gentle hush of overcast,
A cozy glow, shadows are cast.
Raindrops dance on soft green grass,
Embracing moments that slowly pass.

Underneath the blanket of gray,
Hearts find solace in muted play.
The world feels close, and time stands still,
Wrapped in warmth, we feel the thrill.

Colors of Joy

Bright petals burst in vibrant cheer,
A symphony of shades draws near.
Laughter mingles in the breeze,
Nature's palette, all hearts appease.

Children chase the butterflies,
Underneath expansive skies.
Each moment glimmers, pure and bright,
As joy unfolds in radiant light.

Twilight's Patchwork

As twilight spills its dusky charm,
Colors blend without alarm.
A patchwork quilt of night and day,
Stars begin their gentle sway.

The moon peeks through with silver grace,
Casting dreams on time's embrace.
Whispers linger in the air,
A world transformed, beyond compare.

Canvas of the Sun

Golden rays paint the sky,
A dance of light so free,
Whispers of warmth draw nigh,
Nature's glorious decree.

Clouds become a soft hue,
As colors merge and sway,
Each moment feels brand new,
In the warmth of the day.

Embracing the Brightness

With open arms I stand,
Basking in morning's grace,
Beams of light touch the land,
A smile upon my face.

Every shadow fades away,
As hope begins to rise,
In the glow of the day,
I find my heart's true size.

Luminous Journey

Step by step, we ignite,
Path of vibrant delight,
Stars guide us through the night,
With dreams that burn so bright.

Each footfall brings us near,
Wonders waiting in line,
Together, we persevere,
On this journey divine.

Hues of Happiness

In fields of colors wide,
Joy blooms in every glance,
With laughter as our guide,
We twirl in life's sweet dance.

A spectrum of pure glee,
Painting moments we share,
Together, you and me,
In this vibrant affair.

The Loom of Morning's Glow

In silence the loom begins to weave,
Threads of pastel hues as daylight cleaves.
Soft whispers of dawn in every strand,
Crafting tapestries at nature's hand.

Golden rays dance on the fabric's face,
A gentle touch, a warm embrace.
Each color blooms in morning's grace,
Looming dreams in this sacred space.

Light-Touched Textiles of Tomorrow

Fabrics glisten, kissed by light,
Threads that shimmer, delicate and bright.
Patterns emerge, stories untold,
Woven futures in colors bold.

Every stitch a promise made,
Echoes of hopes that never fade.
Textiles whisper of journeys new,
In the loom, a vision grew.

Embroidery of Day's First Breath

As dawn awakens, a canvas is born,
Stitching together the veil of morn.
With gentle hands, the sun does trace,
Embroidery fine on nature's face.

Threads of gold entwine with dew,
As day embarks with colors anew.
Every detail a promise tight,
In the soft embrace of morning light.

Warmth Sewn into the Fabric of Life

In each layer, warmth is found,
Stitched with love, both soft and sound.
Fabrics hold what hearts desire,
Knit with dreams, each thread a fire.

Colors mingled in harmony true,
The fabric of life is me and you.
With every seam, a tale to tell,
In the warmth of love, we dwell.

Soft Light of Dusk

The sun sinks low, a gentle sigh,
Whispers of evening fill the sky.
Soft shadows dance, the world takes rest,
In dusky hues, we are all blessed.

Stars begin to twinkle bright,
Emerging from the cloak of night.
Moonlight bathes the earth in grace,
A perfect calm, a tender space.

Timeless Glow

A fire burns with steady flame,
Embers glow and call our name.
In warmth we find our stories told,
Timeless moments, rich as gold.

Each flicker sparks a memory,
Of laughter shared, of love set free.
In golden light, we find our way,
Through twilight's embrace, we choose to stay.

A Tapestry of Colors

Fields of blossoms stretch and sway,
Nature's brush paints night and day.
Vibrant hues in harmony,
A canvas woven, wild and free.

In every petal, dreams unfold,
A story whispered, bright and bold.
Together we weave, hand in hand,
A tapestry across the land.

Glow of the Heavenly Weave

Stars are diamonds in the night,
A heavenly weave of purest light.
Each thread a wish, a silent prayer,
Illuminating paths we dare.

In the cosmos, we find our place,
The glow of dreams, a soft embrace.
Together we journey, hearts alight,
Guided by the stars' gentle sight.

Light Weaving Through the Leaves

Sunlight dances on the trees,
Whispers of nature in the breeze.
Shadows flicker, softly play,
Colors mingling through the day.

Each leaf a canvas, painted bright,
Nature's art in morning light.
Golden rays in emerald hue,
A symphony of life anew.

A Canvas of Warm Mornings

Painting dreams on dawn's embrace,
Gentle warmth in every space.
Birds awaken, songs resound,
In the quiet, joy is found.

Sunrise spills its golden kiss,
Each moment feels like pure bliss.
Brushstrokes of the waking sky,
Wrap the world as day draws nigh.

Glimmers in Threads of Nature

Softly woven, nature's thread,
Sparkling jewels where pathways spread.
A tapestry of earth and sky,
Underneath the clouds that fly.

Rivers glisten, laughter flows,
Woven tales in petals' close.
Each heartbeat, nature's song,
In the fabric, we belong.

Radiant Horizons of Fabric Dreams

Dreams unfold at day's first light,
Horizons beckon, future bright.
Stitched with hope in vibrant seams,
Life's a canvas, full of dreams.

Colors burst as day awakes,
Through the fabric, heaven breaks.
Voices whisper, gentle streams,
Weaving thoughts in radiant beams.

Day's Embrace

Morning light breaks through the haze,
Softly warming the earth's cool face.
Birds begin their sweet morning song,
Nature stirs as the day grows strong.

Gentle breezes whisper low,
Welcoming dreams where rivers flow.
Colors bloom in vibrant cheer,
As the world awakens here.

In the skies, the sun ascends,
Promising light that never ends.
Each moment holds a new chance,
Life unfolds in a bright dance.

With open arms, the day invites,
Guiding hearts towards new heights.
In every heartbeat, every breath,
We find the joy that conquers death.

A Dance of Shadows

In the twilight, shadows play,
Dancing lightly at end of day.
Whispers echo through the night,
Fleeting forms in silver light.

The moon casts a gentle glow,
While the stars begin their show.
Figures twirl in the cool night air,
Secrets hidden, none aware.

Every rustle speaks of fate,
Glimmers beckon, oh, so late.
In the play of shade and light,
We lose ourselves to the night.

As we glide through velvet dreams,
Reality is not what it seems.
In the dark, we lose our care,
In the dance, we breathe the air.

Glimmers of Hearth

Underneath a starlit sky,
Flickering flames dance and sigh.
Stories shared in warm embrace,
Light that sparks in every face.

The hearth glows with memories dear,
Echoes of laughter fill the sphere.
In each spark, a tale unfolds,
A tapestry of life retold.

Comfort found in fragile light,
Binding hearts through the night.
With each flame, we find our way,
Glimmers of hope, come what may.

As the embers softly wane,
Love remains through joy and pain.
In the hush of twilight's glow,
We find warmth in all we know.

Sunshine's Gentle Caress

Waking softly to a golden hue,
Sunshine spills on skies so blue.
Petals stretch to greet the dawn,
Nature wakes, and life goes on.

Every ray a tender touch,
Whispers softly, oh so much.
Light that dances on the ground,
In its warmth, peace can be found.

Through the leaves, a playful breeze,
Bringing laughter with such ease.
In every smile, the sun's embrace,
Fills the heart with purest grace.

As the day fades into night,
We hold on to that soft light.
In our dreams, the sun will stay,
Guiding us along the way.

Morning's Melody

The sun spills gold upon the dew,
Birds begin their joyful tune,
Whispers of a day anew,
Nature dances 'neath the moon.

Breezes carry softest sighs,
Leaves in chorus start to sway,
As shadows melt beneath the skies,
Morning lights the path of day.

Nature's Quilt

Fields adorned in colors bright,
Stitching dreams with every thread,
Mountains wrap in robes of white,
A tapestry where hearts are led.

Winding rivers trace the seams,
Sunsets whisper warmth and rest,
Here in nature, life redeems,
Each corner of the earth feels blessed.

Patterns in the Air

Clouds drift softly, shapes unfold,
Stories in their shadows play,
As the winds in laughter scold,
Dreams take flight, then drift away.

Kites soar high in vibrant hues,
Whirling leaves in swirling dance,
Nature's play, a grand amuse,
In the sky, our spirits prance.

Reflections of Radiance

Mirrors of the water gleam,
Sunset's brush paints skies afire,
Each ripple holds a fleeting dream,
Echoes of a heart's desire.

Stars appear in twilight's embrace,
Glistening on the evening tide,
In their light, we find our place,
With love and hope, we gently glide.

Threads of Dawn's Embrace

In the hush before the day,
Whispers of the night decay.
Softly rays begin their climb,
Kissing earth with gentle rhyme.

An orchestra of colors blend,
Where shadows and the light extend.
Threads of gold, a canvas vast,
Embracing futures, weaving past.

Each petal wakes, adorned in dew,
Nature's brush, a vibrant hue.
Hope unfurls in every beam,
Chasing dreams, igniting gleam.

Together now, the world awakes,
In every heart, a promise bakes.
Threads of dawn, in tender grace,
We find our purpose, we find our place.

Golden Weaves of Daybreak

Morning's breath, a gentle sigh,
Stitches through the azure sky.
Golden weaves of light arise,
Beneath the canvas, dreams devise.

Nature's loom spins tales anew,
Promises held in every view.
Fields of light, like rivers flow,
Guiding hearts where hopes can grow.

Seasons shift, yet warmth remains,
In every heart, in joy, in pains.
Daybreak paints with vibrant care,
Golden threads are everywhere.

Together in this sacred space,
We gather strength, we seek our place.
Golden weaves, a gift bestowed,
In the light of love, we're sowed.

Fabrics of Radiant Whispers

Nightingale's soft serenade,
In every corner, shadows fade.
Fabrics weave in shades so bright,
Radiant whispers greet the light.

Threads of silver, patterns rare,
Dance beneath the sunlit air.
Each connection warmly sewn,
Binding hearts, and seeds we've sown.

Stories etched in night's embrace,
Fraying edges leave a trace.
Fabrics swirling, tales to tell,
In radiant whispers, we dwell.

Every moment intertwined,
In the tapestry, love's designed.
Together, we shall find our song,
Fabrics of life, where we belong.

Tapestry of Light and Warmth

In the dawn, a tale unfolds,
Tapestry in colors bold.
Light and warmth make shadows dance,
As we step into this chance.

With each thread, we find our way,
Guiding us through night and day.
Moments shared, a vibrant hue,
Tapestry we weave anew.

Hearts converge, like stars align,
In the beauty, sweet and fine.
Together, every dream ignites,
Tapestry of love in flight.

In the silence, whispers start,
Binding souls, a work of art.
Together we will always stand,
Tapestry of life, hand in hand.

Embers of Daybreak

The sun breaks through the misty veil,
Golden rays begin to sail,
In the silence, whispers swell,
Spirits rise where shadows fell.

Birds take flight, a dance so sweet,
Nature wakes to vibrant beat,
Each leaf sparkles, kissed by light,
A canvas turns from dark to bright.

Morning's breath, a gentle sigh,
Promises of warmth draw nigh,
Beneath the sky, a story spun,
From ashes bright, a new day begun.

With every flicker, hope does grow,
Embers fade, the world aglow,
In the heart, a flame will stay,
Guiding us along the way.

Tapestry of Dawn

Threads of color interlace,
In the dawn, a soft embrace,
Fingers drawn to sky's vast art,
Woven dreams that touch the heart.

Every hue begins to blend,
Nature's song, a sweet commend,
Pastel skies and living streams,
A masterpiece of waking dreams.

As the sun begins to rise,
Filling earth with gold, surprise,
Tapestry of life unfurls,
In the dawn, the magic swirls.

We stand still, in awe, amazed,
By the beauty life has phrased,
In this moment, hope will dawn,
A brand new world waits to be drawn.

Radiant Whispers

In the hush of breaking morn,
Softly shine, the dreams reborn,
Radiant whispers in the air,
Every heartbeat, every prayer.

Gentle breezes carry songs,
Where the light and love belong,
Echoes tender, sweet and clear,
In the silence, truth draws near.

As the world awakens slow,
Magic sparkles, starts to flow,
With each thought, a world created,
Boundless love, never fated.

Radiant whispers dance on high,
In the stillness, let us fly,
In the glow of day's embrace,
Find the warmth, our sacred place.

Loom of Light

In the loom where shadows play,
Light weaves threads of bright array,
Each filament, a story told,
In the warmth, a heart of gold.

Golden silk and silver strands,
Creating dreams with gentle hands,
Time stitched close with every thread,
Whispering what lies ahead.

Colors merge in vivid hue,
Life's own fabric, bright and true,
Moments captured, woven tight,
In the loom, we find our light.

Every fabric holds a tale,
In the weave, we will not fail,
As we journey, day by day,
In the loom of light, we'll stay.

Fabricated Dreams of Endless Light

In shadows cast, the whispers play,
A dance of hope, a bright array.
With every turn, the visions gleam,
Fabricated dreams, a waking dream.

Through corridors, where echoes roam,
We chase the glint of light we own.
Each step a spark, each breath a flare,
Endless light guides us through the air.

A tapestry of starry nights,
With threads of gold and silken sights.
We weave our wishes, bold and bright,
In fabricated dreams of endless light.

The heart ignites, a fiery blend,
Where hope and fear do twist and bend.
In every corner, shadows weave,
A promise held in those who believe.

The Bright Mosaic of Nature's Art.

Amidst the blooms, where colors sing,
A canvas painted by nature's wing.
Each petal soft, each hue a spark,
A bright mosaic, alive, not dark.

The dancing leaves in golden sun,
Whisper of tales, their lives begun.
In gentle winds, their stories spread,
Nature's art, where dreams are fed.

The sapphire skies, the emerald ground,
In every detail, beauty found.
A vibrant dance in perfect grace,
The bright mosaic, nature's embrace.

As seasons shift, the palette changes,
Life's pure rhythm, it rearranges.
Yet in each phase, a path so true,
Nature's art shines, forever new.

Threads of Golden Dreams

In twilight's glow, the threads entwine,
Golden dreams in soft design.
With every stitch, a story's spun,
Woven whispers, two hearts as one.

Through fabric's depths, our futures gleam,
The warmth of love, a gentle theme.
In every fold, in every seam,
The threads of golden dreams redeem.

With careful hands, the tapestry grows,
In patterns rich, as life bestows.
Each thread a memory, bright and bold,
In woven warmth, our dreams unfold.

As night descends, the stars ignite,
In fields of hope, they shine so bright.
Together woven, we rise and beam,
In threads of golden dreams, we dream.

Woven in Warmth

In cozy nooks, where shadows mix,
Warm blankets hold our secrets fixed.
Each stitch a love, each fold a cheer,
Woven in warmth, we draw you near.

By crackling fires, our stories weave,
In tales of joy, we dream and believe.
The warmth embraces, the night unfolds,
In woven dreams, our hearts hold gold.

The threads of time in hues of grace,
Through laughter's echo, we find our place.
With every whisper, each gentle sigh,
Woven in warmth, our spirits fly.

As dawn approaches, the light will blend,
In vibrant colors, our paths extend.
Together wrapped, in love's bright charm,
We flourish strong, forever warm.

Fleeting Warmth

In the sun's soft glow, we find our grace,
Moments cherished, none can replace.
Whispers of laughter, a gentle breeze,
Time slips away, like leaves from trees.

Golden rays dance upon the grass,
Each fleeting glimpse, we wish would last.
Hearts ignite with the simplest spark,
Embracing warmth as daylight departs.

The evening chill beckons us near,
Fading light, yet we hold it dear.
Memories linger as shadows grow,
In fleeting warmth, love's ember flows.

With twilight's kiss, the day must end,
Though moments fade, our hearts will mend.
In every heartbeat, the warmth remains,
Forever cherished, amidst the rains.

Flickers of Joy

Little sparks in the night sky,
Moments woven, oh so spry.
Laughter dances in the air,
Joyful whispers everywhere.

Each heartbeat sings a sweet refrain,
Echoes of love that softly sustain.
Like stars that twinkle, bright and bold,
Flickers of joy in stories told.

In gentle smiles and playful tease,
Finding light in times that please.
Every laughter a gentle spark,
Illuminating the softest dark.

Life's brief moments, a canvas spun,
Brushstrokes of joy, but never done.
Fleeting glimpses of what we hold,
Flickers of joy, forever gold.

Daylight's Embrace

Awake to the sun's warm glow,
Promises of light in the morning flow.
Each ray a hug from the sky,
Inviting dreams as the days pass by.

Fields awaken, colors bloom,
Nature's canvas dispels the gloom.
With every dawn, a chance to rise,
Daylight's embrace, a sweet surprise.

Whispers of hope dance in the air,
A melody soft, inviting care.
Hands held tight as shadows fade,
In daylight's warmth, love is laid.

As evening approaches, the sun dips low,
In daylight's embrace, we come to know.
Each moment precious, a gentle trace,
Captured eternally in daylight's grace.

Warm Horizons

Horizon glows with the setting sun,
A canvas painted, day is done.
Colors bleed into night's soft veil,
Warmth of twilight, a tender trail.

As day surrenders, stars awaken,
Promises whispered, none forsaken.
Hearts beat softly, dreams take flight,
On warm horizons, bathed in light.

Each moment stretches, time stands still,
Embracing warmth against the chill.
The world aglow in amber hues,
Warm horizons infuse our views.

In every journey, we find our way,
Through dusk and dawn, come what may.
With open hearts and endless skies,
Warm horizons hold our sighs.

Kaleidoscope of Heat

Waves of bright colors swirl and play,
Crimson and gold in the dance of the day.
Each hue a story, vibrant and sweet,
In the kaleidoscope, warmth lies at our feet.

Sunbeams flicker through shifting frames,
A flickering fire that softly claims.
Each turn reveals a new, warm scene,
In this vivid spectrum, we are serene.

Fires of summer, bold and alive,
Breath of the sun, where dreams take a dive.
The world is a canvas, a brilliant display,
Painted with passion, in joyous array.

As night draws close, colors fade,
Yet in our hearts, the warmth won't shade.
For in every pulse, a memory stays,
A kaleidoscope of heat that always plays.

Golden Stitches of Hope

Stitched in the fabric of dreams untold,
Threads spun from courage, woven in gold.
Every knot a promise, every seam a guide,
In the quilt of our lives, love rests inside.

Sunshine peeks through the clouds of despair,
Each flicker of light, like a gentle prayer.
With every heartbeat, we gather the thread,
Sewing together the paths we once tread.

The warmth of connection, stitched tight and clear,
In golden fibers, we conquer our fear.
Hope is the needle that mends the fray,
Crafting a tapestry that leads our way.

With every sunrise, a new stitch is made,
In the quilt of tomorrow, our fears will fade.
Hold on to those stitches, they will not break,
For within their embrace, we find what we make.

Harmony in Daylight

Morning light dances on dew-kissed leaves,
Nature awakens, as gently she weaves.
Birds sing a chorus, a melody sweet,
In harmony's cradle, the world finds its beat.

Soft whispers echo through the cool air,
Sunlight spills gold, with warmth to share.
In every heartbeat, a rhythm unfolds,
Tales of connection, in silence retold.

Together we bask in the arms of the day,
Embracing the moments, come what may.
As shadows grow long, we hold on tight,
In the gentle embrace of the fading light.

Harmony lingers where hearts intertwine,
A symphony played in a world so divine.
So let us rejoice in each moment so bright,
Finding our solace in daylight's delight.

Threads of Radiance

Woven together in a dance of light,
Threads of radiance shimmer, pure and bright.
Every color a whisper, soft and serene,
Stitching the dreams that chase through the green.

In the tapestry vast, we find our place,
Intertwined journeys, the fabric of grace.
With every small stitch, a bond we create,
Connecting our stories, sealed by fate.

Under the stars, these threads intertwine,
Crafting a legacy, simply divine.
Holding each moment, a treasure to keep,
In the heart's quiet chamber, where shadows sleep.

Radiance dances through laughter and tears,
Threads of our past defy all our fears.
In each woven smile, life finds its way,
Threads of radiance shining every day.

Sunbeam Stitches Across the Sky

Bright sunbeams thread the blue,
Weaving warmth where dreams take flight.
Clouds drift softly, whispers true,
Kissing earth with gentle light.

In the canvas painting wide,
Nature's brush creates a show.
Every hue blooms, feelings bide,
As day unfolds, we watch it grow.

Golden threads of time unwind,
Moments stitched with ease and grace.
Each sunrise a treasure we find,
In the sky, our hopes embrace.

As dusk descends, the colors blend,
A tapestry of night begins.
With every twilight's soft descend,
Day's last breath, the magic spins.

Custom-Made Mornings of Gold

Whispers of dawn in hues so bright,
Awaken dreams, embrace the day.
With every ray, the world ignites,
In warm embrace, we find our way.

Custom-made with light and air,
Each morning draws us to the sun.
Woven moments, joy we share,
With golden threads, our day's begun.

Hearts united, hopes entwined,
In this fabric of shared time,
Magic lingers, love defined,
In every beat, a quiet rhyme.

When evening falls, we save the light,
Remembering the gold we wore.
In memories, those days so bright,
Live forever, an open door.

Papercut Shadows and Light

Shadows dance in flickering hues,
Papercut stories in the night.
Every shape a tale imbues,
In fleeting glances, pure delight.

Light falls softly, carving grace,
With every edge, a story told.
Laughter echoes in this space,
As dreams unfold, both brave and bold.

Severed pieces on the floor,
Reflecting journeys, paths we tread.
Each cut reveals, opens a door,
In shadows deep, we find our thread.

As hours pass, the edges blur,
In twilight's grasp, we breathe anew.
Papercut shadows softly stir,
A world reborn, with every cue.

Heartstrings of Golden Threads

With every heartbeat, we connect,
Threads of gold intertwine and weave.
In laughter shared and peace checked,
A tapestry of love we leave.

Stitching moments, soft and fine,
Through trials faced and joys revealed.
With every thread a story lines,
In our hearts, the wounds are healed.

Golden strings that bind our souls,
In gentle pulls, our spirits soar.
Together we mend, we play our roles,
Creating homes, we each explore.

The fabric of life, rich and warm,
A quilt of dreams, through night and day.
In each embrace, a quiet charm,
Heartstrings dance in love's array.

Harmony Under the Sun

Beneath the sky, we come alive,
With laughter shared, our spirits thrive.
In gentle breezes, joy takes flight,
Together, we bask in golden light.

Mountains echo our sweet refrain,
In nature's arms, we feel no pain.
Harmony flows through every sound,
In unity, our hearts are bound.

As colors blend in sunset's glow,
We find our place, let friendship grow.
The sun sets low, but love remains,
Creating bonds where peace sustains.

In days of warmth, our souls entwine,
Each moment savored, sweet as wine.
With open arms, we greet the day,
In harmony, we choose to stay.

Dreams in the Daylight

In daylight's grasp, our visions soar,
With every dream, we seek for more.
Awake, we chase what hope can bring,
In vibrant hues, our spirits sing.

The world unfolds, a canvas bright,
Each step we take ignites the light.
With courage bold, we dare to dream,
In every heart, a vibrant gleam.

Awake the dawn, embrace the sun,
With every heartbeat, we have won.
Boldly we stand, our dreams in sight,
In daylight's kiss, we find our flight.

With eyes wide open, we take the leap,
Into the wonders, our souls shall keep.
In every moment, magic's spun,
Our dreams awaken under the sun.

Festival of Light

Amidst the stars, the lanterns rise,
A dance of dreams lights up the skies.
With every flicker, hope ignites,
In this festival, pure delight.

Colors swirling, laughter flows,
As every face in joy bestows.
Together we stand, hands interlaced,
In glowing warmth, the years embraced.

The night is young, let music play,
In harmony, we find our way.
For every spark that dares to shine,
In this moment, our hearts align.

As shadows fade, we hold the light,
With love and peace, the world feels right.
In this magic, we come alive,
In our hearts, the joys survive.

Celestial Fabric

Woven threads of night and day,
In cosmic dance, the stars will sway.
Galaxies spin in timeless grace,
In endless space, we find our place.

The moon whispers secrets, calm and clear,
In twilight's embrace, we draw near.
Each comet's tail, a wish in flight,
In celestial dreams, we find our light.

Through storms of fate, we sail the skies,
With every moment, new hope lies.
In starlit realms, our spirits roam,
In this vastness, we find our home.

As dawn breaks forth with gentle sigh,
We carry dreams that soar and fly.
In fabric woven from night's deep blue,
The universe sings, and so do we.

Sunlit Embrace

The morning light spills gold,
Awakening the dew,
Whispers in the gentle breeze,
Nature's soft, sweet cue.

Golden rays dance in trees,
Casting shadows on the ground,
With every breath I take,
Joy and peace abound.

Clouds drift lazily by,
Painting stories in the air,
In this sunlit embrace,
Love's warmth everywhere.

As day turns into dusk,
Colors blend and play,
In the heart of the moment,
I choose to stay.

Textures of the Horizon

The sky is a canvas wide,
With hues from dusk till dawn,
Colors swirling in a tide,
A masterpiece reborn.

Mountains rise with strength profound,
Soft valleys cradle dreams,
Ready for the sight unbound,
Where nothing's as it seems.

Waves crash upon the shore,
Nature's rhythm in each line,
Stories of the ocean's roar,
In textures, they entwine.

Birds soar high with grace,
Tracing paths in the blue sky,
In every fleeting space,
Life's beauty flying by.

Weaving the Sky

Threads of light entwine,
In a tapestry so grand,
Creating an endless line,
Woven by nature's hand.

The sun and moon converse,
In a dance of day and night,
Casting shadows, they disperse,
Leaving us with pure delight.

Stars flicker like soft dreams,
Guiding wishes from below,
Illuminate the night it seems,
With a gentle, loving glow.

Every heartbeat echoes high,
In the silence of the vast,
We are threads beneath the sky,
Connected to the past.

Luminescent Journey

Through a forest filled with light,
I wander, lost in thought,
Every step a soft delight,
In glow of dreams so sought.

The fireflies dance in pairs,
Creating sparkles in the night,
Drawing warmth from tender stares,
Their flickers shine so bright.

The moon reflects a path ahead,
Guiding souls with silken beams,
In every whisper that is said,
Echoes of our shared dreams.

Adventure calls me on,
With each heartbeat, I can feel,
This luminescent dawn,
In every pulse, it's real.

Light's Gentle Caress

Morning whispers soft and sweet,
Sunrise paints the earth's heartbeat.
Each ray a touch, a warm embrace,
In dawn's light, we find our place.

Shadows fade with golden spills,
Hope awakens, softly thrills.
Nature dances, vibrant, free,
In light's glow, we learn to be.

Gentle streams of amber weave,
In every sigh, we start to believe.
A canvas bright with colors bright,
In the morn, we find our light.

Hold the warmth within your soul,
Let the light make you whole.
For in these glimmers, we will see,
The beauty of what we can be.

Mosaic of Glimmers

Each fragment shines, a tale to tell,
In colors bright, they weave so well.
Scattered jewels of fate and chance,
In the moments, we find our dance.

Broken pieces come alive,
In every corner, dreams survive.
A patchwork quilt of heart and mind,
Through light's lens, the truth we find.

Glimmers spark in night's embrace,
Reflecting hopes in timeless space.
A million stories, bright and bold,
In this mosaic, life unfolds.

With every glance, we see the glow,
United in warmth, we learn and grow.
Together standing side by side,
In harmony, our hearts abide.

Sunlit Dreams

In the meadow where shadows play,
Sunlit dreams chase clouds away.
Every beam a path we tread,
In golden hues, our spirits fed.

Whispers of warmth, a gentle guide,
Through fields of light, we walk with pride.
Each heartbeat synced with nature's song,
In sunlit realms, we all belong.

The horizon beckons with open arms,
In daylight's grace, we find our charms.
Moments linger, sweet and rare,
In sunlit dreams, we breathe the air.

Hold onto visions, let them soar,
As shadows dance upon the floor.
With every sunrise, hopes ignite,
In our hearts, we hold the light.

Rays of Connection

In each ray, a story spun,
A bond that's forged, two become one.
Through laughter shared and tears cried,
In radiant light, we find our guide.

Hands entwined, together strong,
In rays of warmth, we both belong.
With every heartbeat, souls align,
In this glow, our spirits shine.

Moments flicker, bright and fair,
In gentle whispers, we declare.
The ties that bind us never break,
In rays of love, for our own sake.

With open hearts, we journey forth,
In light's embrace, we find our worth.
Together in this cosmic dance,
Let's cherish each and every chance.

The Gold in Between

In shadows cast by ancient trees,
Whispers float on the evening breeze.
They carry tales of love and strife,
Finding gold in the heart of life.

Glimmers shine in the darkest night,
Hope ignites like stars so bright.
Each moment missed, each chance we find,
Is treasure buried within the mind.

Through every crack, the light will seep,
Awakening dreams from their deep sleep.
In every silence, every sigh,
We hold the gold that cannot die.

So seek the moments, soft and sweet,
In laughter's echo and lovers' meet.
The true worth lies in what we glean,
In the precious gold that's in between.

Children of the Light

We dance beneath a sky so wide,
With stars above and hearts as guides.
We are the children of the light,
Chasing dreams that soar in flight.

In every laughter, in every tear,
We weave a tale that draws us near.
Together strong, we rise and shine,
In love's embrace, our souls entwined.

Through valleys low and mountains tall,
We hear the whispers, heed the call.
In gentle kindness, we find our way,
Lighting the path, come what may.

So let us share this radiant glow,
As children of the light, we grow.
Hand in hand, we'll write our story,
In unity, we find our glory.

Echoes of Warmth

In the quiet corners of the night,
Where shadows dance and stars ignite.
Soft murmurs rise like whispered prayer,
Echoes of warmth linger in the air.

Through pages worn and tales retold,
Fragments of love in the years of old.
Each heartbeat's rhythm, a story sings,
As time unveils the joy that clings.

In gentle hugs and tender smiles,
We weave the moments into miles.
A tapestry of shared embrace,
Holding close every cherished face.

So let the echoes flow and sway,
In every breath, in every day.
For warmth resides in hearts that care,
As echoes of love linger everywhere.

Canvas of the Cosmos

Upon the canvas, vast and deep,
The cosmos whispers, secrets to keep.
Each twinkling star, a story told,
In hues of silver, blue, and gold.

Planets dance in cosmic waltz,
In a rhythm that never halts.
Galaxies swirl in graceful flight,
A masterpiece crafted in the night.

We are but painters with dreams to cast,
In strokes of wonder, futures vast.
With hearts as brushes, spirits free,
We color the canvas of eternity.

So gaze upon the starlit scene,
And find the magic where we've been.
In every blink, the cosmos sings,
A canvas alive with endless things.

Sun-Kissed Hues of Serenity

The morning glows with golden light,
A gentle breeze, as soft as night.
Whispers of warmth in the lavender fields,
Nature's embrace, the soul it yields.

With every beam, the shadows play,
In sun-kissed hues, we find our way.
The sky, a canvas, painted bright,
Cradles dreams in the calm daylight.

Petals flutter, a dance so free,
Colors mingle in harmony.
In every hue, a story we find,
Echoing peace, soothing the mind.

As day unfolds, the world awakes,
With sun-kissed hues, our spirit breaks.
In serenity's glow, hearts reside,
In nature's arms, we find our guide.

Illuminated Patterns of Joy

Laughter blooms where shadows fade,
In radiant light, sweet memories made.
Patterns unfold, bright and bold,
Stories of joy in colors told.

Sparkling dreams in every glance,
Life dances in a vibrant trance.
With each step, a rhythm found,
In illuminated joy, hearts resound.

The sun dips low, the twilight sings,
In every chord, a joy life brings.
United we stand, hand in hand,
In patterns of warmth, we understand.

Under the stars, the laughter flows,
In illuminated nights, our spirit grows.
Every heartbeat, a song to play,
In patterns of joy, we light the way.

Woven Dreams Under Bright Skies

Threads of hope in daylight spun,
Woven dreams, our hearts are one.
Under bright skies, we chase the stars,
In the fabric of life, we mend the scars.

Tale of love in each stitch tight,
Crafted gently by morning light.
Colors entwined, a vision clear,
In woven dreams, we conquer fear.

The clouds above, like whispers glide,
With every wave, our spirits ride.
Hands together, we weave our fate,
Under bright skies, we celebrate.

In the tapestry of endless night,
Every thread shines, a beacon bright.
Together, we rise, our spirits roam,
In woven dreams, we find our home.

Rays of Hope in Fabric Form

In every thread, a story glows,
Rays of hope in fabric flows.
Stitched with care, each moment sewn,
A tapestry of dreams well known.

With every fold, a promise lies,
In vibrant hues, like sun-lit skies.
Rays of hope dance on the seam,
Together they weave, a radiant dream.

In the quiet night, when shadows creep,
The fabric holds what we long to keep.
Hope wrapped tight, in layers warm,
In every stitch, new worlds form.

Woven together, hearts align,
In rays of hope, our futures shine.
So let us forge, through storm and calm,
In fabric's embrace, we find our balm.

Sun-Kissed Sequins

In the morning glow we dance,
Glistening under sunlight's chance,
Each sequin sparkles, bright and bold,
Whispers of warmth and stories told.

Waves of gold upon the skin,
Laughter echoes, we begin,
A tapestry of shimmering hues,
Creating dreams, the world imbues.

With footsteps light, we twirl and sway,
In this moment, we can play,
Sun-kissed magic in the air,
A celebration, free and rare.

As daylight fades, the colors blend,
To twilight's hues, we now descend,
Sequins fall like stars at night,
Our hearts aglow with pure delight.

Fabric of Morning Glories

Petals unfold to greet the dawn,
Nature's fabric, softly drawn,
With hues of blue and shades of pink,
A gentle sigh, a whispered wink.

In the garden, laughter sways,
As sunlight spills its golden rays,
Morning glories reach for sky,
In their beauty, time slips by.

Leaves entwined in tender grace,
Nature weaves its warm embrace,
With every breath, the world awakes,
A symphony, the heart partakes.

As day unfurls, the colors blend,
The fabric holds, yet will not bend,
In each bloom, a story starts,
The morning sings, it fills our hearts.

Illuminated Patterns

Shadows dance on the wall,
In flickering light, they rise and fall,
Patterns woven with day and night,
In every corner, dreams take flight.

Glow of lanterns, soft and warm,
Crafting stories in quiet form,
Each reflection holds the past,
In illuminated patterns cast.

With whispered tales, the night unfolds,
Resilient hearts, as the world beholds,
Connections made in twilight's grace,
A shimmer found in every space.

In the stillness, we close our eyes,
Underneath the starry skies,
Embracing patterns, vast and grand,
Illumination, hand in hand.

Chasing the Light

In the morning's gentle haze,
We chase the light, in playful ways,
With open hearts, we dare to dream,
In every shadow, hope will gleam.

Across the fields, we run so free,
With laughter ringing, you and me,
The sunlight dances on our skin,
A fleeting moment, pure within.

As daylight slips towards the night,
We gather memories, holding tight,
Each ray a whisper, soft and bright,
In every heart, we chase the light.

With dreams alight, we take our flight,
To places where our spirits unite,
Together shining, pure and true,
In every moment, me and you.

Portrait of the Aether

In the canvas of the sky, so vast,
Whispers of winds and shadows cast.
Stars like diamonds softly gleam,
Nature weaves its silent dream.

Colors blending, day and night,
Mountains cradle the fading light.
In every stroke, the cosmos sings,
Tales of old in the aether brings.

Clouds parade in gentle grace,
Time unfurls in this sacred space.
Echoes of a world unseen,
A vast expanse, serene, pristine.

Beneath the stars, our souls align,
In the stillness, we trace the line.
Eternity holds its breath, it seems,
In the portrait spun from dreams.

Embodied Warmth

In a cozy nook, the fire burns bright,
Embracing hearts in its gentle light.
Laughter dances around the flame,
Each shared moment, never the same.

Soft whispers linger in the air,
Wrapped in comfort, love laid bare.
Hands entwined, we find our peace,
In this warmth, all worries cease.

Fireside stories, memories spun,
Rekindling joy, two souls as one.
With each crackle, our dreams ignite,
In the glow, everything feels right.

As shadows play against the wall,
We find our solace, hear the call.
The world outside may roar and fight,
But here, we bask in embodied light.

Vibrant Mosaic

In gardens where the colors bloom,
Nature's palette dispels the gloom.
Petals whisper tales untold,
In vibrant hues, their beauty bold.

Butterflies flit on jeweled wings,
Serenading life, the joy it brings.
Each flower a note in a grand design,
A mosaic of moments, perfectly aligned.

Raindrops glisten like crystal beads,
Nourishing the earth and sprouting seeds.
A tapestry woven with sun and rain,
Creating a world where life remains.

In this vibrant dance of earth and sky,
We find ourselves, we learn to fly.
Each hue, each note, a sacred piece,
In the vibrant mosaic, we find our peace.

Luminance in Nature

Morning dew on blades of grass,
Sparkles catch the light as they pass.
Sunrise spills like molten gold,
Illuminating stories untold.

Trees embrace the warming rays,
In their shadows, the stillness stays.
Birds awaken with joyful song,
Nature's voices, harmonious and strong.

Mountains stand in majestic form,
Guardians of light, through calm and storm.
Streams of silver dance and flow,
Reflecting the world, a gentle show.

In the heart of nature's grace,
We find our place, we know our space.
Luminance guides us, pure and true,
In every moment, life feels new.

Glowing Moments

In twilight hues, we find our way,
Whispers of dreams that softly play.
Each laugh a spark, igniting the night,
Together we dance in pure delight.

Memories woven in gentle smiles,
Time slips softly, stretching for miles.
With every heartbeat, love's gentle tune,
We shine bright beneath the moon.

A fleeting glance, the world feels right,
Moments captured, a glimpse of light.
In each soft gaze, a promise shared,
In glowing moments, we're always bared.

Through life's quick turns and sudden bends,
With you, my love, the journey transcends.
Hand in hand, we forge our fate,
In glowing moments, we celebrate.

Warmth in Every Thread

In every stitch, a tale unfolds,
Patterns of love in hues so bold.
Each thread a memory, tightly spun,
Warmth in every strand, we are one.

From frayed beginnings, we craft anew,
A tapestry rich in every hue.
Silken whispers, promises made,
In every fabric, love won't fade.

Joyful colors, hand in hand,
In the embrace of a woven land.
Through storms and sunshine, we persist,
Warmth in every thread, we exist.

A gentle pull, a calming sway,
Together we're woven, come what may.
In life's great loom, we find our bliss,
Warmth in every thread, a timeless kiss.

Brilliant Threads

In a world of colors, vibrant and bright,
Brilliant threads weave patterns of light.
Stitch by stitch, dreams come alive,
In the fabric of hope, we will thrive.

From golden dawn to twilight's grace,
Each thread a story, a silken embrace.
Together we stitch, a quilt of love,
With every layer, blessings from above.

Through every challenge, we spin our fate,
Creating bonds that will never abate.
In the tapestry of life, we find our way,
Brilliant threads light up the day.

With hands entwined, we craft a maze,
A journey of warmth, in countless ways.
In the art of weaving, we take flight,
Brilliant threads guide us through the night.

The Light Beyond Shadows

When the night whispers and the world grows still,
There's a glimmer of hope, a quiet thrill.
Beyond the shadows, where dreams take flight,
We chase the dawn, a beacon of light.

With every heartbeat, the shadows flee,
In the warmth of courage, we find the key.
Together we rise, hand in hand,
The light beyond shadows helps us stand.

Life's gentle whispers, soft and clear,
Guide us through darkness, dispelling fear.
In the dance of dawn, our spirits soar,
The light beyond shadows forevermore.

So let us wander where shadows may creep,
With hearts aglow, and dreams to keep.
In unity, we stand, braving the cold,
The light beyond shadows, a story told.

Nature's Golden Needlework

Golden threads weave through the trees,
Sunlight dances on the leaves.
Birdsong flutters in the air,
Nature's art is beyond compare.

Rivers stitch the land with grace,
Mountains rise, a proud embrace.
Flowers bloom in vibrant hues,
Nature's needlework imbues.

Clouds drift softly overhead,
Whispers of earth, where dreams are fed.
Every petal, every stone,
In this tapestry, we're not alone.

Breezes carry secrets told,
In the forest, stories unfold.
Nature's hands, so deft and kind,
In her needlework, peace we find.

Warm Threads of Celestial Harmony

Stars weave softly in the night,
Threads of warmth, a gentle light.
Moonbeams touch the earth below,
Celestial symphony in flow.

Each twinkle sings of dreams anew,
Harmony in shades of blue.
Galaxies in graceful dance,
Bound together by fate's chance.

Planets rotate, a silent tune,
Kissed and cradled by the moon.
In this vast, unending space,
We find our truth, our rightful place.

Warm threads bind us, soul to soul,
In this grand and timeless whole.
Celestial bodies intertwine,
A cosmic quilt, forever divine.

The Fabric of Day's Embrace

Sunrise paints the world anew,
Golden rays, a hopeful hue.
Each dawn wraps the earth in light,
A fabric spun, warm and bright.

Clouds drift lazily, soft and white,
Stitching shadows with pure delight.
Fields awaken, colors grow,
In this embrace, life starts to flow.

Rays of warmth caress the skin,
A gentle hug from deep within.
Moments woven, thread by thread,
In daylight's fabric, we are led.

As dusk approaches, hues entwine,
A closing stitch, the day divine.
In the fabric, memories keep,
Hearts and dreams in timeless sleep.

Threads of Light in the Evening

As twilight weaves its gentle thread,
Stars awaken, sweetly spread.
Eve's soft whispers fill the air,
Threads of light, beyond compare.

Shadows dance on grassy knolls,
Nature sighs as daylight folds.
The horizon glimmers and fades,
In evening's quilt, serenity wades.

Moonlight casts a silver glow,
Illuminating paths we know.
Each twinkling light, a guiding star,
Threads of hope, no matter how far.

In the calm, our spirits rise,
Underneath the starlit skies.
Threads of light unite the night,
Bringing dreams in soft twilight.

Radiance in Motion

Whispers dance on morning air,
Golden rays comb through the trees.
Each leaf glitters, showing flair,
Nature sings its sweet reprise.

Breezes carry laughter high,
Petals twirl in joyful play.
Underneath the vast blue sky,
Life unfolds in bright array.

Sunset paints the world anew,
Crimson strokes across the sea.
In its brilliance, dreams ensue,
Radiance unfurls so free.

Constellations of Light

Night arrives with stars aglow,
Celestial orbs in stillness shine.
Guiding paths for hearts to know,
In the dark, their light divine.

Through the cosmos, whispers flow,
Tales of ancients, stories spun.
Each star's twinkle, tales they sow,
A connection never done.

Galaxies in motion dance,
Waltzing through the velvet sky.
In their glow, we find our chance,
To dream big and wonder why.

Sunbeam Symphony

Morning calls with golden rays,
Notes of warmth begin to swell.
Nature hums in bright displays,
Sunlit chords, a joyful spell.

Through the branches, shadows sway,
Vibrant hues of green and gold.
In this light, our worries fray,
Every moment, sweet and bold.

As the daylight starts to fade,
Chords of twilight gently ring.
With each note, a memory laid,
In the night, our hearts take wing.

Reflections of the Day

In the mirror of the lake,
Clouds drift softly, dreams unfold.
Each ripple tells the tales we make,
Captured moments, stories told.

Sunlight lingers on the shore,
Whispers of the evening breeze.
Nature's canvas, evermore,
Painting life with effortless ease.

As the stars begin to peek,
The world wraps in twilight's sigh.
In reflections, whispers speak,
Carrying the day goodbye.

Threads of Inspiration in Daylight

In the morning's gentle light,
Ideas weave in pure delight.
A tapestry of thoughts takes flight,
As shadows fade into the bright.

Colors blend, the mind expands,
Crafting dreams with trembling hands.
Each moment a thread, each breath a chance,
To dance with life in a vibrant trance.

Nature whispers in soft tones,
As seeds of wisdom find their homes.
With every glance, a story grows,
Unraveling mysteries that time bestows.

Threads of inspiration softly spin,
An endless journey deep within.
Beneath the sun where hopes reside,
We find the courage to abide.

Gilded Stitches of Nature's Hand

Underneath the sapphire sky,
Nature crafts her art so high.
Golden hues in every strand,
Gilded stitches of her hand.

Mountains rise with steep embrace,
Rivers carve a timeless grace.
Flowers bloom in colors bold,
Stories in their petals told.

The forest hums a tune so sweet,
With whispers that are soft and fleet.
Each leaf, a note within the weave,
In nature's quilt, we all believe.

As seasons turn and colors fade,
Her stitched design will never jade.
In every glance, a world divine,
In the gilded threads, our hearts align.

The Quilt of Dawn's Radiance

Dawn unfolds with tender grace,
A quilt of light in every space.
Threads of gold and crimson glow,
Stitching dreams where shadows flow.

The sky awakens, painted bright,
Banishing the veil of night.
Each ray a promise, soft and clear,
In the quilt of dawn, hope draws near.

Whispers ride on morning's air,
Memories woven with utmost care.
Nature yawns in vibrant hues,
As the day unveils its views.

With every breath, a new refrain,
In the quilt of dawn, joy will reign.
A melody of warmth and light,
Blessings echo through the bright.

Sunlit Patterns on the Horizon

Over hills where shadows play,
Sunlit patterns greet the day.
Each ray a brushstroke on the field,
Where nature's wonders are revealed.

In the distance, colors blend,
A canvas where the day extends.
Clouds drift by with gentle ease,
Painting dreams on the morning breeze.

As sunlight spills on leaves of green,
The world awakens, fresh and keen.
Every glance unveils the art,
Of sunlit patterns that touch the heart.

In this dance of light and shade,
Nature's beauty will not fade.
On the horizon, our hopes arise,
As we chase the sunlit skies.